HAL•LEONARD

KULELE

PLAY-ALONG

Tin Pan Alley

T0082010

CONTENTS

Ukulele - Chris Kringel

ISBN 978-1-4803-2439-8

HAL•LEONARD®
CORPORATION

7777 W. BLUEMOUND RD. P.O. BOX 13819 MILWAUKEE, WI 53213

In Australia Contact:
Hal Leonard Australia Pty. Ltd.
4 Lentara Court
Cheltenham, Victoria, 3192 Australia
Email: ausadmin@halleonard.com.au

Visit Hal Leonard Online at
www.halleonard.com

Baby, Won't You Please Come Home

Words and Music by Charles Warfield and Clarence Williams

First note

Verse
Moderately ♩ = 118

1., 3. Ba - by, won't you please come   home,   'cause your mam-ma's all a -
2. *Instrumental*

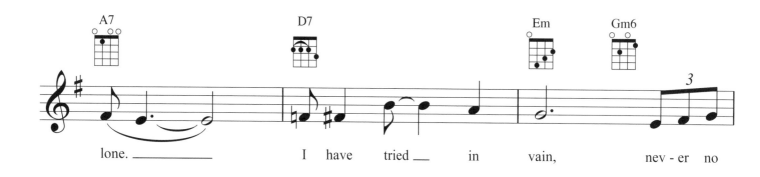

lone. _____   I have   tried ___   in   vain,   nev - er no

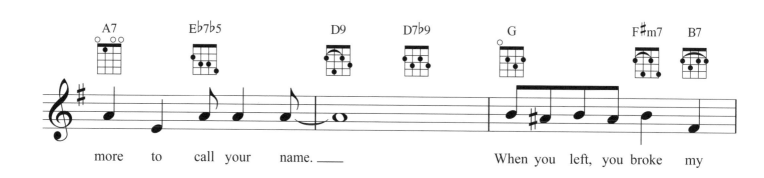

more   to   call   your   name. ____   When you   left, you broke   my

heart _____ be - cause I nev - er thought we'd part. Ev - 'ry

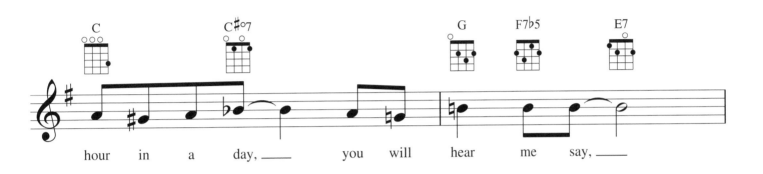

hour in a day, ____ you will hear me say, ____

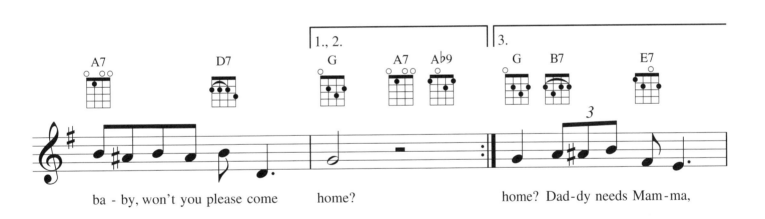

ba - by, won't you please come home? home? Dad-dy needs Mam-ma,

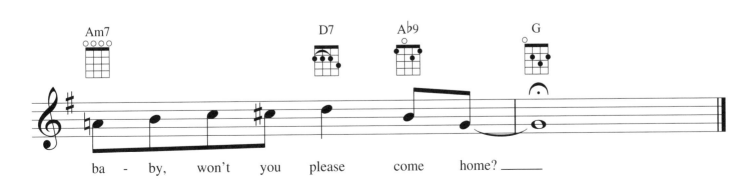

ba - by, won't you please come home? _____

Carolina in the Morning

Lyrics by Gus Kahn
Music by Walter Donaldson

First note

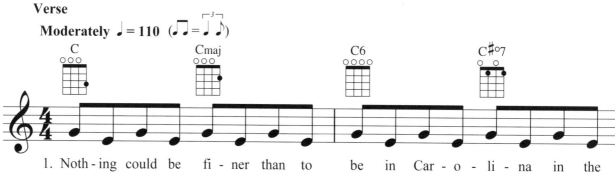

1. Noth - ing could be fi - ner than to be in Car - o - li - na in the
2. Stroll - ing with my girl - ie where the dew is pearl - y ear - ly in the

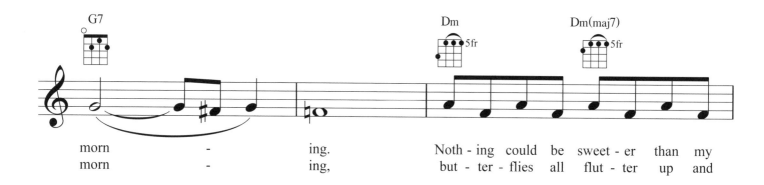

morn - - ing. Noth - ing could be sweet - er than my
morn - - ing, but - ter - flies all flut - ter up and

To Coda ⊕

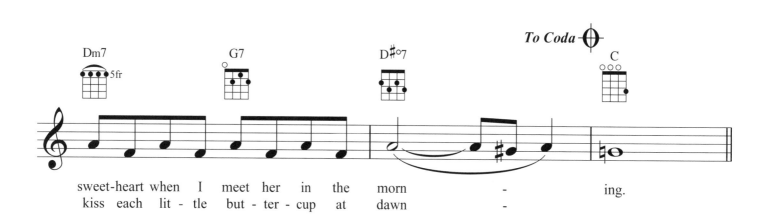

sweet-heart when I meet her in the morn - - ing.
kiss each lit - tle but - ter - cup at dawn -

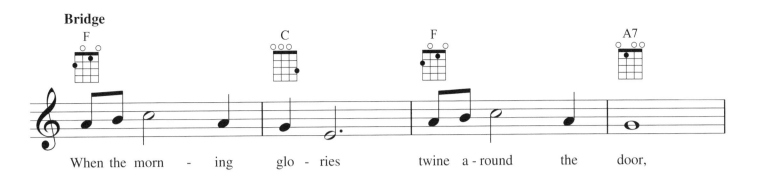

Bridge

When the morn - ing glo - ries twine a - round the door,

D.C. al Coda

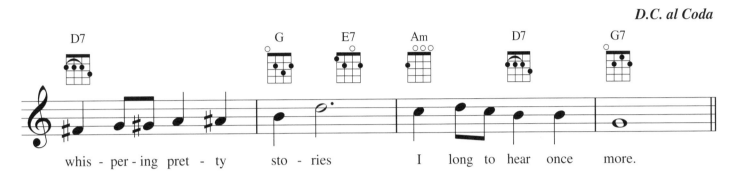

whis - per - ing pret - ty sto - ries I long to hear once more.

Coda

Outro

ing. If I had A - lad-din's lamp for on - ly a day, ___

I'd make a wish and here's what I'd say: ___ "Noth - ing could be fi - ner than to

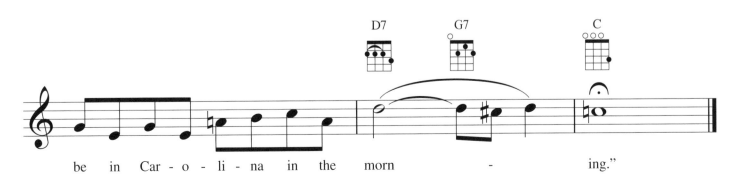

be in Car - o - li - na in the morn - ing."

5

Give My Regards to Broadway

from LITTLE JOHNNY JONES
from YANKEE DOODLE DANDY
Words and Music by George M. Cohan

TRACK 5

First note

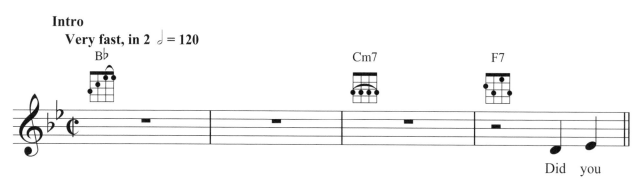

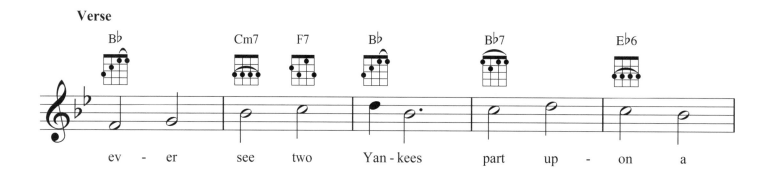

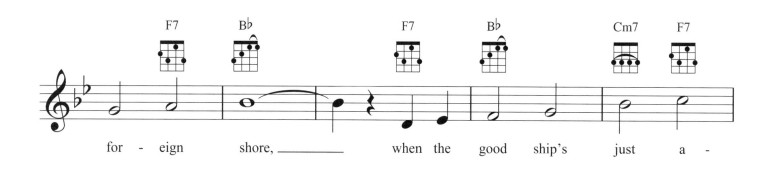

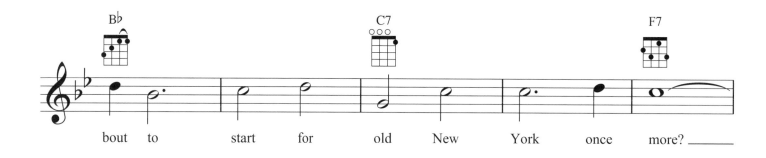

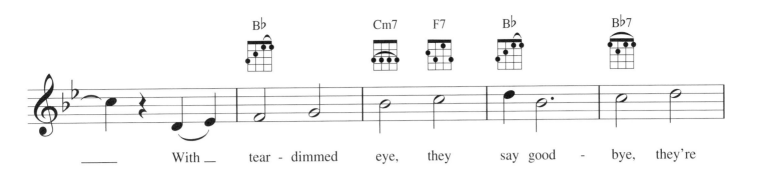

With ___ tear - dimmed eye, they say good - bye, they're

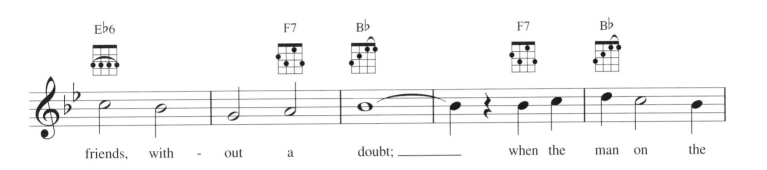

friends, with - out a doubt; _____ when the man on the

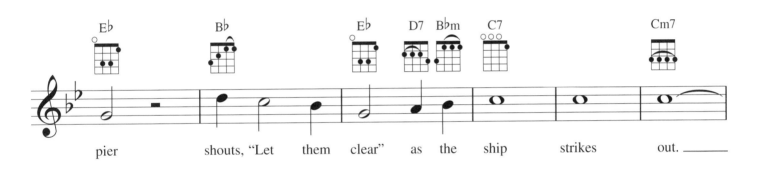

pier shouts, "Let them clear" as the ship strikes out. _____

Chorus

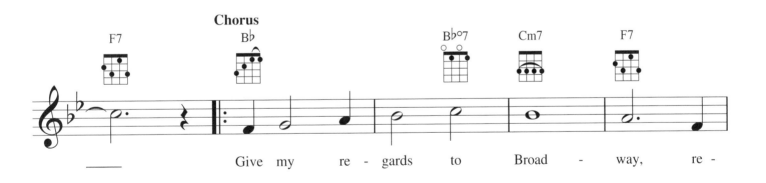

___ Give my re - gards to Broad - way, re -

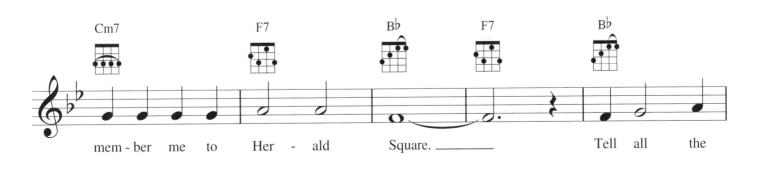

mem - ber me to Her - ald Square. _____ Tell all the

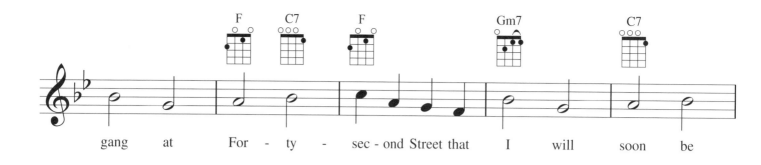

gang at For - ty - sec - ond Street that I will soon be

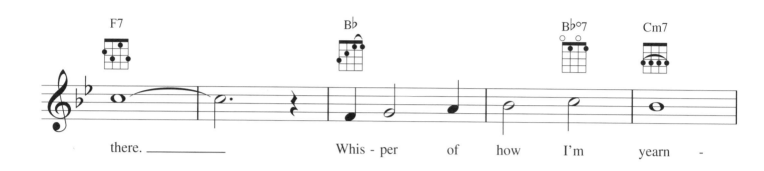

there. _____ Whis - per of how I'm yearn -

ing to min - gle with the old - time throng. _____

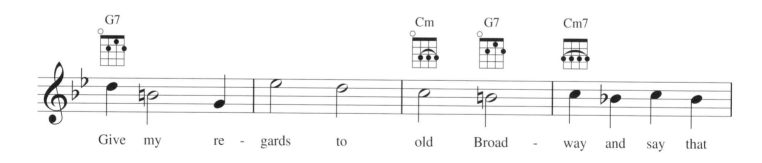

Give my re - gards to old Broad - way and say that

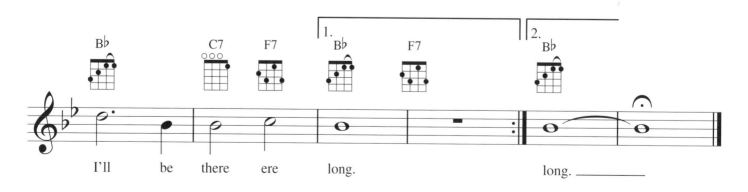

I'll be there ere long.   long. _____

My Melancholy Baby

Words by George Norton
Music by Ernie Burnett

TRACK 9

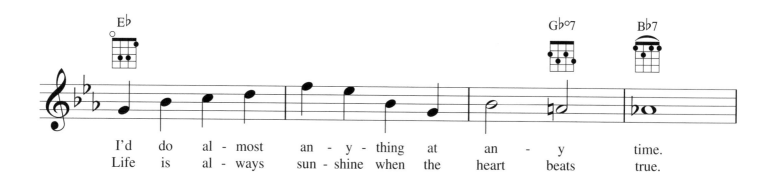

I'd do al - most an - y - thing at an - y time.
Life is al - ways sun - shine when the heart beats true.

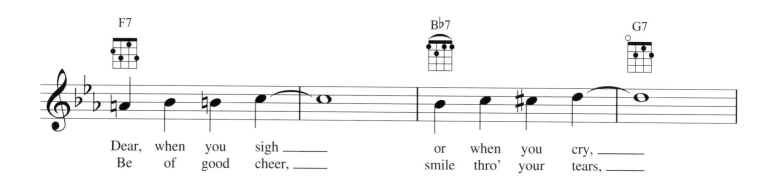

Dear, when you sigh _____ or when you cry, _____
Be of good cheer, _____ smile thro' your tears, _____

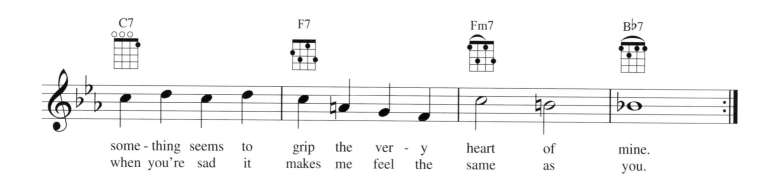

some - thing seems to grip the ver - y heart of mine.
when you're sad it makes me feel the same as you.

Chorus

1. Come to me, my mel - an - chol - y ba - by,
2. *Instrumental*

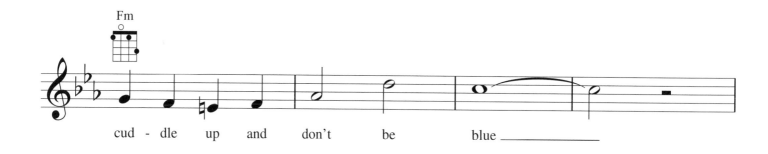

cud - dle up and don't be blue _____

Let Me Call You Sweetheart

Words by Beth Slater Whitson
Music by Leo Friedman

TRACK 7

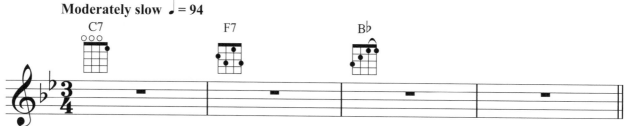

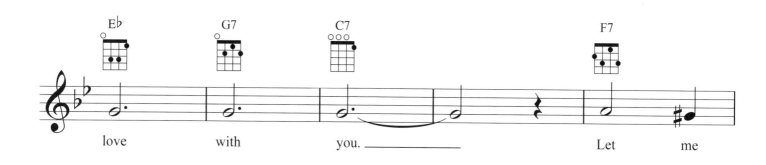

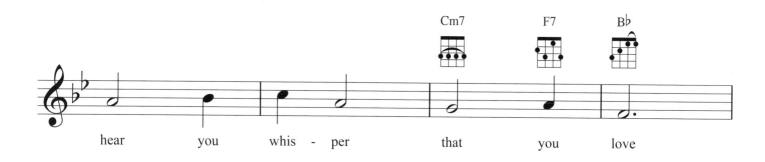

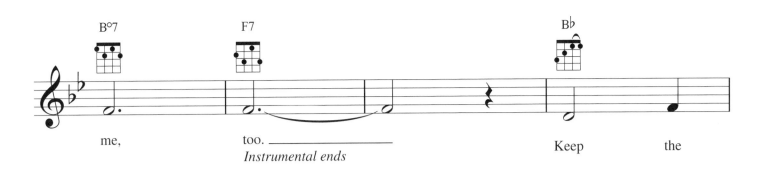

me, too. _____
Instrumental ends

Keep the

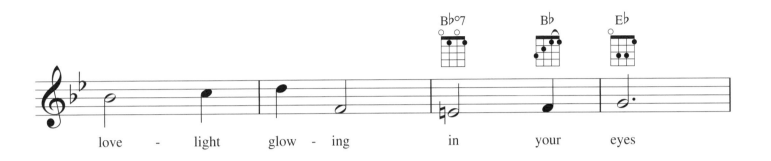

love - light glow - ing in your eyes

so true. _____ Let me

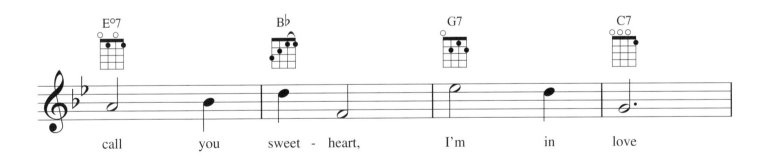

call you sweet - heart, I'm in love

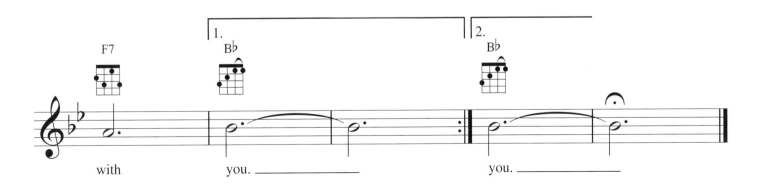

with you. _____ you. _____

Rock-a-Bye Your Baby with a Dixie Melody

from SINBAD

Words by Sam M. Lewis and Joe Young
Music by Jean Schwartz

TRACK 11

First note

Intro

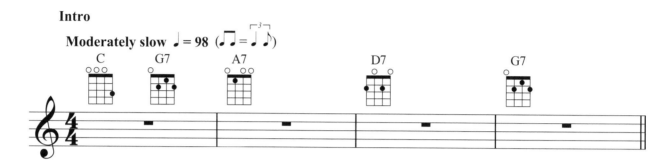

Verse

Mam-my mine, _____ your lit-tle roll-in' stone that rolled a - way, _

strolled a - way. _ Mam-my mine, _____ your roll-in' stone is roll-in'

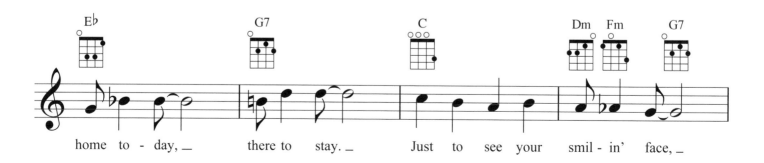

home to - day, _ there to stay. _ Just to see your smil-in' face, _

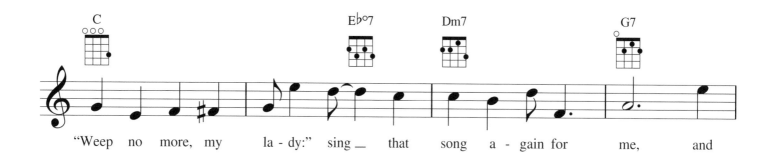

"Weep no more, my la - dy:" sing __ that song a - gain for me, and

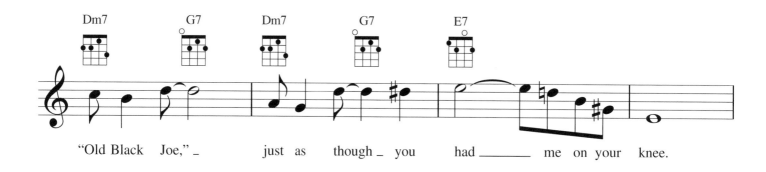

"Old Black Joe," __ just as though __ you had _____ me on your knee.

A mil-lion ba - by kiss-es I'll de - liv - er the min-ute that you sing the

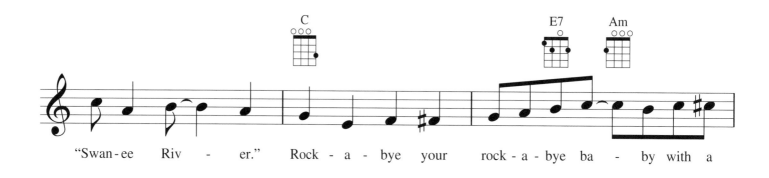

"Swan-ee Riv - er." Rock - a - bye your rock - a - bye ba - by with a

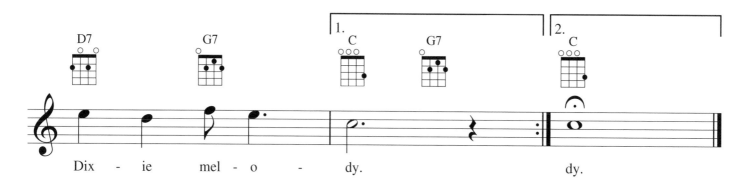

Dix - ie mel - o - dy. dy.

Swanee

Words by Irving Caesar
Music by George Gershwin

First note

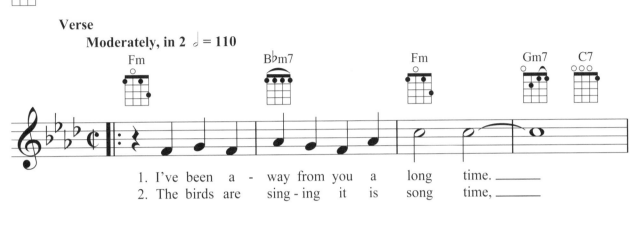

1. I've been a - way from you a long time. _____
2. The birds are sing - ing it is song time, _____

I nev - er thought I'd miss you so. _____ Some - how I
the ban - jos strum - min' soft and low. _____ I know that

feel your love was real, near you I long to
you yearn for me, too, Swan - ee,

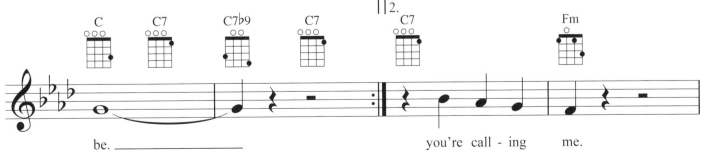

be. _____ you're call - ing me.

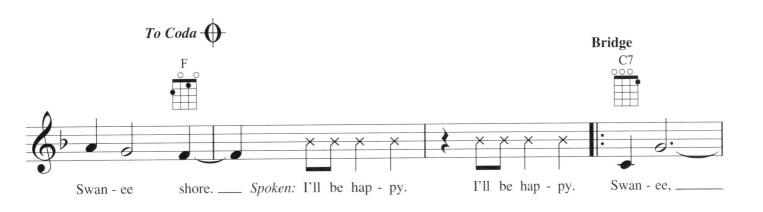

Swan - ee shore. ___ *Spoken:* I'll be hap - py. I'll be hap - py. Swan - ee, ___

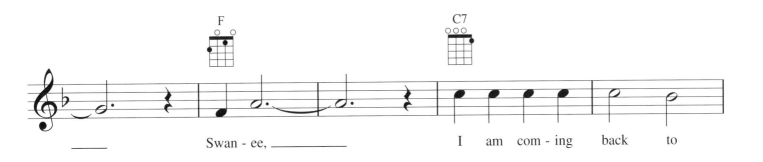

___ Swan - ee, ___ I am com - ing back to

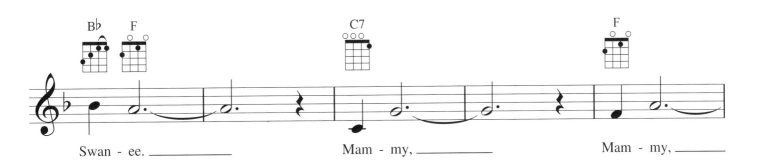

Swan - ee. ___ Mam - my, ___ Mam - my, ___

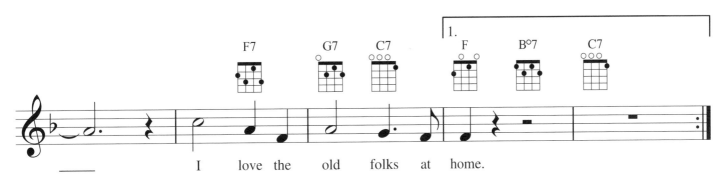

___ I love the old folks at home.

D.S. al Coda

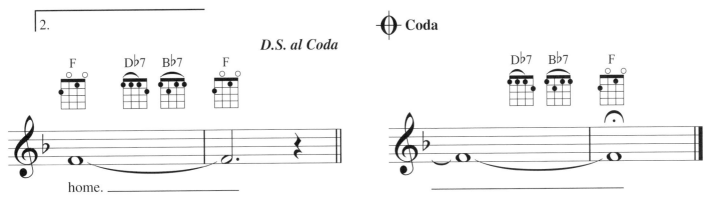

home. ___

When My Baby Smiles at Me

Words and Music by Harry von Tilzer, Andrew B. Sterling, Bill Munro and Ted Lewis

TRACK 15

First note

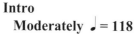

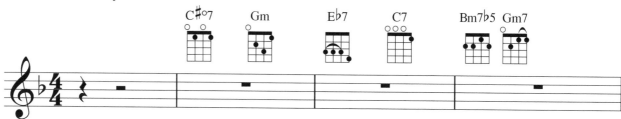

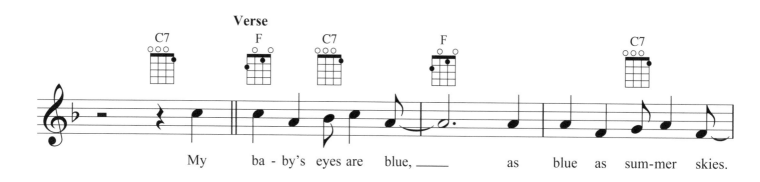

My ba-by's eyes are blue, ____ as blue as sum-mer skies.

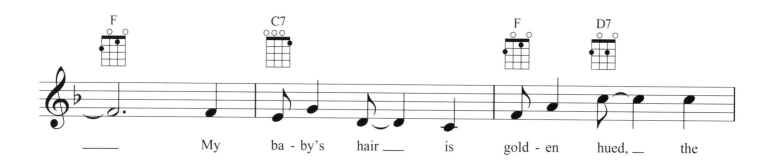

____ My ba-by's hair ____ is gold-en hued, __ the

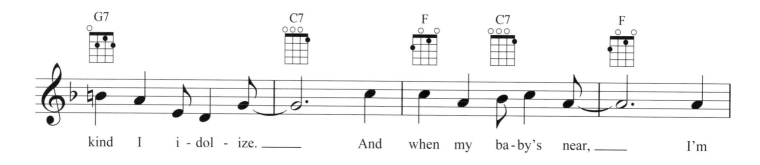

kind I i-dol-ize. ____ And when my ba-by's near, ____ I'm

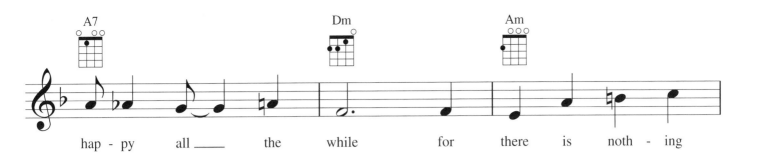

hap - py   all ___   the   while   for   there   is   noth - ing

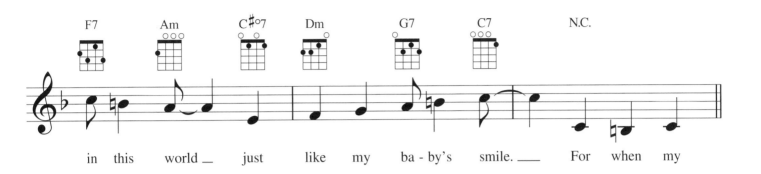

in   this   world ___   just   like   my   ba - by's   smile. ___   For   when   my

Chorus

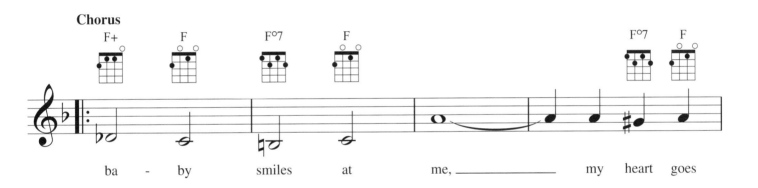

ba - by   smiles   at   me, _____   my   heart   goes

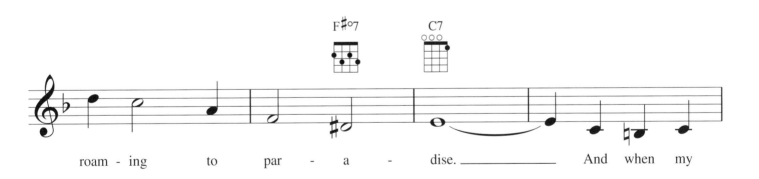

roam - ing   to   par - a - dise. _____   And   when   my

ba - by   smiles   at   me, _____   there's   such   a

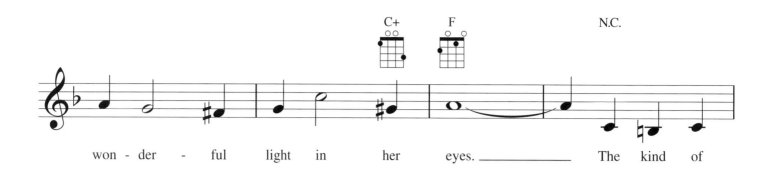

won - der - ful light in her eyes. _____ The kind of

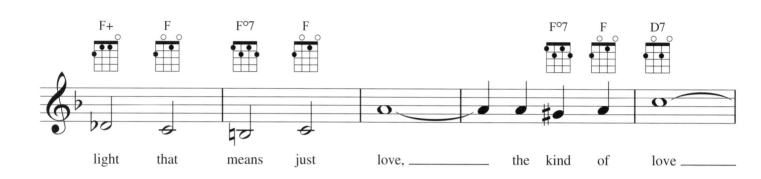

light that means just love, _____ the kind of love _____

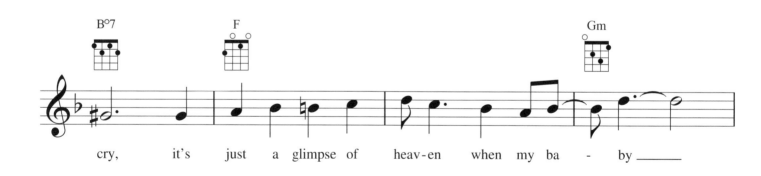

_____ that brings sweet har - mo - ny. I sigh, I

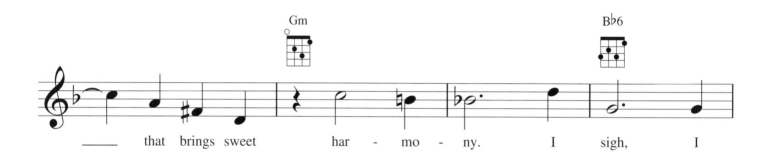

cry, it's just a glimpse of heav-en when my ba - by _____

smiles at me. For when my me. _____

HAL•LEONARD UKULELE PLAY-ALONG

Now you can play your favorite songs on your uke with great-sounding backing tracks to help you sound like a bona fide pro! This series includes the Amazing Slow Downer, so you can adjust the tempo without changing the pitch.

1. POP HITS
00701451 Book/CD Pack $14.99

2. UKE CLASSICS
00701452 Book/CD Pack $12.99

3. HAWAIIAN FAVORITES
00701453 Book/CD Pack $12.99

4. CHILDREN'S SONGS
00701454 Book/CD Pack $12.99

5. CHRISTMAS SONGS
00701696 Book/CD Pack $12.99

6. LENNON & MCCARTNEY
00701723 Book/CD Pack $12.99

7. DISNEY FAVORITES
00701724 Book/CD Pack $12.99

8. CHART HITS
00701745 Book/CD Pack $14.99

9. THE SOUND OF MUSIC
00701784 Book/CD Pack $12.99

10. MOTOWN
00701964 Book/CD Pack $12.99

11. CHRISTMAS STRUMMING
00702458 Book/CD Pack $12.99

12. BLUEGRASS FAVORITES
00702584 Book/CD Pack $12.99

13. UKULELE SONGS
00702599 Book/CD Pack $12.99

14. JOHNNY CASH
00702615 Book/CD Pack $14.99

15. COUNTRY CLASSICS
00702834 Book/CD Pack $12.99

16. STANDARDS
00702835 Book/CD Pack $12.99

17. POP STANDARDS
00702836 Book/CD Pack $12.99

18. IRISH SONGS
00703086 Book/CD Pack $12.99

19. BLUES STANDARDS
00703087 Book/CD Pack $12.99

20. FOLK POP ROCK
00703088 Book/CD Pack $12.99

21. HAWAIIAN CLASSICS
00703097 Book/CD Pack $12.99

22. ISLAND SONGS
00703098 Book/CD Pack $12.99

23. TAYLOR SWIFT
00704106 Book/CD Pack $14.99

24. WINTER WONDERLAND
00101871 Book/CD Pack $12.99

25. GREEN DAY
00110398 Book/CD Pack $14.99

HAL•LEONARD® CORPORATION

7777 W. BLUEMOUND RD. P.O. BOX 13819 MILWAUKEE, WI 53213

www.halleonard.com

Prices, contents, and availability subject to change without notice.

0913

Ride the Ukulele Wave!

The Beach Boys for Ukulele
This folio features 20 favorites, including: Barbara Ann • Be True to Your School • California Girls • Fun, Fun, Fun • God Only Knows • Good Vibrations • Help Me Rhonda • I Get Around • In My Room • Kokomo • Little Deuce Coupe • Sloop John B • Surfin' U.S.A. • Wouldn't It Be Nice • and more!

00701726 . . . . $14.99

The Beatles for Ukulele
Ukulele players can strum, sing and pick along with 20 Beatles classics! Includes: All You Need Is Love • Eight Days a Week • Good Day Sunshine • Here, There and Everywhere • Let It Be • Love Me Do • Penny Lane • Yesterday • and more.

00700154 . . . . $16.99

The Daily Ukulele
compiled and arranged by Liz and Jim Beloff
Strum a different song everyday with easy arrangements of 365 of your favorite songs in one big songbook! Includes favorites by the Beatles, Beach Boys, and Bob Dylan, folk songs, pop songs, kids' songs, Christmas carols, and Broadway and Hollywood tunes, all with a spiral binding for ease of use.

00240356 . . . . $34.99

The Daily Ukulele – Leap Year Edition
366 More Songs for Better Living
compiled and arranged by Liz and Jim Beloff
An amazing second volume with 366 MORE songs for you to master each day of a leap year! Includes: Ain't No Sunshine • Calendar Girl • I Got You Babe • Lean on Me • Moondance • and many, many more.

00240681 . . . . $34.99

Disney Songs for Ukulele
20 great Disney classics arranged for all uke players, including: Beauty and the Beast • Bibbidi-Bobbidi-Boo (The Magic Song) • Can You Feel the Love Tonight • Chim Chim Cher-ee • Heigh-Ho • It's a Small World • Some Day My Prince Will Come • We're All in This Together • When You Wish upon a Star • and more.

00701708 . . . . $12.99

Folk Songs for Ukulele
A great collection to take along to the campfire! 60 folk songs, including: Amazing Grace • Buffalo Gals • Camptown Races • For He's a Jolly Good Fellow • Good Night Ladies • Home on the Range • I've Been Working on the Railroad • Kumbaya • My Bonnie Lies over the Ocean • On Top of Old Smoky • Scarborough Fair • Swing Low, Sweet Chariot • Take Me Out to the Ball Game • Yankee Doodle • and more.

00696068 . . . . $12.99

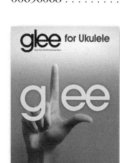

Glee
Music from the Fox Television Show for Ukulele
20 favorites for Gleeks to strum and sing, including: Bad Romance • Beautiful • Defying Gravity • Don't Stop Believin' • No Air • Proud Mary • Rehab • True Colors • and more.

00701722 . . . . $14.99

Hawaiian Songs for Ukulele
Over thirty songs from the state that made the ukulele famous, including: Beyond the Rainbow • Hanalei Moon • Ka-lu-a • Lovely Hula Girl • Mele Kalikimaka • One More Aloha • Sea Breeze • Tiny Bubbles • Waikiki • and more.

00696065 . . . . $9.99

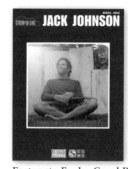

Jack Johnson – Strum & Sing
Cherry Lane Music
Strum along with 41 Jack Johnson songs using this top-notch collection of chords and lyrics just for the uke! Includes: Better Together • Bubble Toes • Cocoon • Do You Remember • Flake • Fortunate Fool • Good People • Holes to Heaven • Taylor • Tomorrow Morning • and more.

02501702 . . . . $10.99

Elvis Presley for Ukulele
arr. Jim Beloff
20 classic hits from The King: All Shook Up • Blue Hawaii • Blue Suede Shoes • Can't Help Falling in Love • Don't • Heartbreak Hotel • Hound Dog • Jailhouse Rock • Love Me • Love Me Tender • Return to Sender • Suspicious Minds • Teddy Bear • and more.

00701004 . . . . $14.99

Jake Shimabukuro – Peace Love Ukulele
Deemed "the Hendrix of the ukulele," Hawaii native Jake Shimabukuro is a uke virtuoso. Our songbook features note-for-note transcriptions with ukulele tablature of Jake's masterful playing on all the CD tracks: Bohemian Rhapsody • Boy Meets Girl • Bring Your Adz • Hallelujah • Pianoforte 2010 • Variation on a Dance 2010 • and more, plus two bonus selections!

00702516 . . . . $19.99

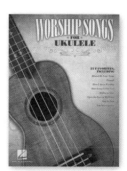

Worship Songs for Ukulele
25 worship songs: Amazing Grace (My Chains are Gone) • Blessed Be Your Name • Enough • God of Wonders • Holy Is the Lord • How Great Is Our God • In Christ Alone • Love the Lord • Mighty to Save • Sing to the King • Step by Step • We Fall Down • and more.

00702546 . . . . $12.99

HAL•LEONARD® CORPORATION
7777 W. BLUEMOUND RD. P.O. BOX 13819 MILWAUKEE, WI 53213

0913

THE CANADIAN BRASS

BOOK OF BEGINNING QUINTETS

Arranged and edited by WALTER H. BARNES

THE CANADIAN BRASS EDUCATIONAL SERIES